Mike Slaughter

The
Hopes & Fears
of All the Years

Down

— TO —

Earth

Are Met in
Thee
Tonight

With
Rachel Billups

Devotions for the Season
by Rachel Billups

Abingdon Press / Nashville

P9-APP-494

Down to Earth
Devotions for the Season

This book is printed on elemental chlorine-free paper.

Library of Congress Cataloging-in-Publication data applied for.

978-1-5018-2344-2

16 17 18 19 20 21 22 23 24 25 — 10 9 8 7 6 5 4 3 2 1
MANUFACTURED IN THE UNITED STATES OF AMERICA

CONTENTS

Week Three: Down to Earth Lifestyle

Week Four: Down to Earth Obedience

INTRODUCTION

It is an honor and a privilege to be walking this Advent journey with you. Not only are we entering into the most wonderful time of the year, but we have an opportunity, as followers of Jesus, to partner together, to actively wait, and to anticipate the birth and coming of Christ our King. Throughout this journey we will discover that Jesus is no ordinary King. His rule and reign are the result of God's strange but comforting down-to-earth love.

I love the way *The Message* describes the Incarnation: "The Word became flesh and blood / and moved into the neighborhood" (John 1:14). Neighborhoods are full of people—churched people and unchurched people, those who are seeking God and those who seem far from God. Perhaps my favorite part of being the church, God's "Plan A" for healing and reconciling the world, is our opportunity to come face-to-face with all kinds of people. And that includes you!

This book is an invitation for us to journey together and ask ourselves the question: how do we become a down-to-earth people?

The very meaning of the phrase "down to earth" calls up a simplicity and ruggedness that challenge our way of living. When the phrase is applied to the practices of love, humility, lifestyle, and obedience, suddenly we realize that this Advent could be the time and space where we live differently. Each year as Advent approaches, we followers of Jesus are called to reorient our daily lives to prepare for the work that God wants to do in us and throughout the world. Perhaps these devotions can serve as a spiritual tool to help us slow our pace and remember the evidence of God's down-to-earth love in our daily lives.

My hope is that these devotions contain more than information; they are intended to start a conversation. The stories included are meant to ignite your creativity and imagination—to help you discover God's presence in your story so that you can join me in exploring God's bigger story.

The devotions are laid out in four weeks. Each week is based on the themes discussed in one of the four chapters of *Down to Earth*, the book written by Mike Slaughter and me. The four themes are down-to-earth love, down-to-earth humility, down-to-earth lifestyle, and down-to-earth obedience. Each week is made up of five devotions, giving the reader flexibility to choose five times during the week to read them. Contained in each devotion are Scripture, comments, and a prayer, giving us time and space to reflect together on God's Word, wrestle with the experience of it, and prayerfully ask God to move us to action.

Most of the devotions involve stories, and stories are meant to be shared. Maybe you are a parent or grandparent and these devotions are simple enough to read to your children or grandchildren. Maybe you can discuss them with a friend over a cup of coffee or hot chocolate. Or maybe you know someone who has never experienced God's down-to-earth love and would find in these devotions some refreshing signs of God in the everyday. As you read, invite others to join you in the conversation.

Friends, God chose to become flesh and blood and move into our neighborhood. It was a terribly earthy thing to do. May these devotions inspire you and me to participate actively in God's down-to-earth mission in our parts of the world.

Rachel Billups

Week 1

Down to Earth
Love

1.

CRANK

Therefore if you have any encouragement from being united with Christ, if any comfort from his love, if any common sharing in the Spirit, if any tenderness and compassion, then make my joy complete by being like-minded, having the same love, being one in spirit and of one mind.

(Philippians 2:1-2)

As we step into this Advent journey together, the question that Paul asks his followers in Philippi—and, by extension, you and me—is this: "Has following Jesus made any real difference in your life?"

Several years ago I worked for ODOT, the Ohio Department of Transportation. I was a flagger, one of those people who hold up road signs. It didn't pay much, but it got me through the gaps when I was in seminary. On the final day of working for ODOT, I was given trash pickup duty, which meant I had an official excuse to drive the entire county for the day and look for trash and dead animals along the road. We never worked alone, and so I was given a partner for the day. His name was Crank.

Crank was kind of a crazy kid, didn't talk much, and seemed to smoke a lot of pot, but I enjoyed his company. As we were traveling through the county we drove near the church where I was serving and I said to Crank, "Hey that's my church!"

Crank looked at me, looked at the church, and said, "Your church?"

"That's right," I said. "I'm the pastor of that church." It was part of my seminary responsibilities.

Crank was real quiet. Then, without trying to hurt my feelings, he said, "Pastor? I didn't even know you were a Christian."

Ouch! I had spent months with Crank, and yet he had no idea I was following Jesus, let alone leading a whole flock of people in following Jesus.

I could have made excuses, maybe assumed he was smoking a little extra that morning, but there was no denying Crank's meaning: "I don't see the difference Jesus is making in your life."

This may be the most wonderful time of the year—when folks sing Christmas carols, show up to kids' plays, and come to worship celebrations on Christmas Eve—but if there's no evidence that Jesus is making a difference in our lives, then those who spend time with us will move on, because of the lack of Jesus they see in you and me.

That moment with Crank changed me. I committed myself to proclaim Jesus not just with my lips but with my life. Following Jesus is not about the season's greetings we share, the cups of eggnog we drink, or even what church we attend; following Jesus is about living a down-to-earth love that makes a difference in our lives and the lives of others.

Crank and I spent the rest of the afternoon picking up trash and getting to know one another's stories. I discovered a young man with dreams and aspirations for the future. And what Crank heard was the story of a sinner saved by grace, who continues to allow God to mend her broken pieces back together.

Lord Jesus, throughout this Advent season shape us with your love. Pour your spirit deep into our hearts and minds, so that we can share with those around us your down-to-earth love. In your name. Amen.

2.

LESSONS LEARNED BY A DECEMBER BABY

Do nothing out of selfish ambition or vain conceit. Rather, in humility value others above yourselves, not looking to your own interests but each of you to the interests of the others.

(Philippians 2:3-4)

I couldn't believe it. They were throwing a birthday party for me.

You have to understand, I was born on December 19, just six days before we celebrate the birthday of Jesus. If you have a December birthday or are close to someone who does, you can feel my pain. I spent years getting gifts that were marked "Happy Birthday" and "Merry Christmas" on the same tag. Because of my December birthday, I could remember only two parties my family had ever thrown for me—one when I turned seven, the other when I turned eleven.

But I didn't grow up resentful. I just understood that Jesus' birthday was bigger than mine, and that fact brought my birth and my life into focus. In fact, being a December baby has given me a sort of spiritual advantage. We live in a culture in which we are told Christmas is all about us: what we want, what our families desire, and what we can materially gain around the holidays. Without even realizing it, being born in December has been a yearly reminder that, although my life matters, it is God's work that brings real significance and meaning to it. It's as if inherent in my birthday is the reminder that this life is not all about me—that ultimately I was made for relationship with God and with other people. As my coauthor and friend Mike Slaughter says, "Christmas is not your birthday."

But this year was different. Even though I was an adult—married with a child—my mom planned a birthday party for me. The party was nothing huge, just a few family and friends, but it was for me. I was honored and excited. It wasn't about the gifts or the cake. It was the fact that, for once, Jesus' birthday did not trump mine.

Yes, it turned out to be a happy birthday, and yes, I remembered that Jesus' birthday is more important. But that cake surely did taste good.

Throughout the month of December there are constant reminders of God's down-to-earth love for the world, from decorations on store shelves to the carols we sing in worship. The entire month is enveloped in a warm sense of genuine joy. It's a time in our culture where creation invites us to a whole new way of living: a life of actively waiting for God's gifts and promises. The month seems extraordinarily special. And although as a December baby I may feel a little shortchanged from time to time, I also feel incredibly honored to celebrate a birthday in the month when we anticipate the coming of the King of kings.

Jesus, Christmas is not my birthday; it is yours! Pour your down-to-earth love over us so that we can be the people you have called and claimed us to be. In your sweet name. Amen.

THE GIFT OF WAITING

A voice of one calling: / "In the wilderness prepare / the way for the LORD; / make straight in the desert / a highway for our God. / Every valley shall be raised up, / every mountain and hill made low; / the rough ground shall become level, / the rugged places a plain."

(Isaiah 40:3-4)

On Mother's Day weekend, I found myself grumbling through a Saturday evening worship celebration. I was not feeling well. In fact, I thought I was going to puke at any moment. It was not the flu. I did not have a virus. But that all-too-familiar wave of nausea was not going away anytime soon. I was preaching, and I was pregnant.

I knew this was just the first of a whole series of weekends where I would feel like I could toss my cookies at any moment, and I was frustrated. "Come on," I thought to myself. "Isn't morning sickness supposed to be relegated to the morning?" But I knew better. This was my fourth pregnancy and the fourth extended season of nausea as a result of being with child.

Annoyed, I prayed, "God, why do I have to feel this way? Why can't I be over this already?" Waiting is not always easy, particularly for those of us achiever types who have agendas for every minute of the day.

Within moments of my prayer, the thought came to mind, "Why are you whining? Have you forgotten the miracle I am growing inside of you?"

Suddenly I realized how terribly bratty I was being. God was birthing a miracle inside me! In hoping that this pregnancy could be different from the rest, I had lost perspective.

I can imagine that God's people, the Israelites, felt that way for centuries. In the pain of oppression, they too nearly lost hope. In their waiting for a messiah, they had grumbled and become discouraged. And yet, God was preparing to birth a miracle that would change not just one woman but the whole world—God's "Plan A" for the salvation of the world, wrapped in a human womb, complete with morning sickness and all.

Sometimes I'm quick to criticize the Israelites for their cantankerous attitude, but then I realize it took a lot less than hundreds of years to turn my faith into frustration. Pregnancy is a physical reminder that miracles take time, that life has to grow, and that actively waiting is not always comfortable or pain-free. Perhaps you too struggle to wait: for employment, for a clean bill of health, for evidence of God's work in your life. But throughout this Advent season, God is inviting us not only to wait actively for the King of kings, but also to wait for God to birth a new miracle in us.

I anticipate witnessing miracles during the Christmas season—with the coming of our fourth child, and with God's down-to-earth love birthed in and through a people who have actively waited for Jesus to arrive.

I wonder what miracle God could be wanting and willing to birth through you.

God of new life and light, help us to wait actively, not with grumbling and complaining, but with anticipation and awe of your life-giving work in our lives and throughout the world, in Jesus' name. Amen.

4.

DON'T YOU WANT MY BREAD?

"If your brother or sister sins, go and point out their fault, just between the two of you. If they listen to you, you have won them over."

(Matthew 18:15)

Conflict—it's a part of all our lives. Although many of us try to avoid it, it's something each of us has to navigate.

A few years ago, my husband and I lived across the street from a guy named Bill. Bill was not the friendliest of neighbors, spent most of his time indoors, and did not participate in any neighborhood activities. Bill did not bother us, and we did not bother Bill—that is, until we parked too close to Bill's mailbox.

When anyone, pastor included, parked too close to Bill's mailbox, he would call the cops and have the cops politely ask to have the vehicle moved. Mind you, these calls usually came on Sunday afternoons. First of all, there was no mail being delivered at that time, and second, we were usually having Bible study. So you can imagine the scene: the Billups' house is full of people studying God's word. Suddenly there is a knock on the door, and who should appear but a police officer in full uniform including his weapon. I know that in some parts of the world Bible study is deemed a dangerous activity, but not in our sleepy, suburban cul-de-sac.

Frustrated and frankly a little offended, we would have people move their cars; but like many neighbors in conflict, we passively avoided addressing the situation. Each Sunday, as people continued to park too close to Bill's mailbox, we continued to move the cars without addressing the issue.

Finally I thought to myself, "I know how to fix this—with food." Food always makes things better. So I baked my world-famous (okay, maybe just cul-de-sac-famous) zucchini bread and took a piping-hot loaf over to Bill. This would surely break the tension between Bill and my family. As I walked across the street, I said a little prayer: *Sweet Jesus, help me to be nice.* And I knocked on Bill's door.

At first there was no answer, but then I heard someone moving around. A moment later, the latch clicked and the door swung open.

"What do you want?" asked Bill.

"I baked you zucchini bread," I said.

Bill looked at me, looked at the bread, and then, barely getting out the words before slamming the door, bellowed, "I don't want your bread!"

Shocked, I stood with bread in hand, thinking to myself, *You don't want my bread? How could anyone not want my bread?*

A few days later, I learned that even though Bill didn't want my bread, he apparently wanted to talk. He wandered over to our yard and gave my husband an earful concerning his view of the neighborhood and the world. We learned that Bill had spent years caring for his aging mother and putting his life on hold. He longed for a time when his life had been simpler and easier, a time when everything seemed to go his way.

It turned out that Bill wasn't looking for bread; he just wanted someone to listen. It made me wonder how many conflicts could be avoided or addressed if we were just willing to listen.

Of course, if listening doesn't work, there's always zucchini bread.

Lord Jesus, help us to address conflict with listening ears and an open heart. In your holy name. Amen.

5.

LOVE DOES

But a Samaritan, as he traveled, came where the man was; and when he saw him, he took pity on him.

(Luke 10:33)

Being part of a church like Ginghamsburg sometimes can lead people to believe doing big things for God is all that matters. Certainly twelve years of investing millions of dollars into Sudan, South Sudan, and Dayton could give one the impression that we followers of Jesus are called to go big or go home at the holidays. But I wonder, in the midst of that big miracle, if we sometimes forget that each miracle begins small—a single act of sacrifice, which is then multiplied by God.

You'd think that Advent and Christmas would be a season when people would be more willing to give and give generously than any other time of the year, but so often the giving that happens around Christmas feels more like charity than it does compassion and mercy. True compassion and mercy are costly, and I'm not talking about writing a check.

In the story we know as the good Samaritan, Jesus reminds us that love knows no boundaries. The Samaritan is despised—a half-breed, a person rejected by the religious faithful—and yet the Samaritan is the hero of the story. For the Samaritan shows mercy and compassion, not only by writing a check (paying for all the medical expenses of the man injured) but also by going out of his way to make sure the man is restored to health. The Samaritan's actions are simple: clean a wound, rent a room, come back to check. And yet these simple actions save the man's life. Too often during Advent and Christmas we forget that small acts of compassion and mercy have as much potential to change lives as Christmas Miracle offerings.

It's the small things that make a difference: the neighbor who clears snow from the elderly couple's driveway, the family that bakes cookies and takes them to the local nursing home (and not just at Christmas), the woman who knits blankets for each new child in the congregation, the man who changes the oil in a single mom's car. These gifts seem small, but when multiplied with God's love they have the power to change lives.

Last year, a friend of mine decided to use Christmas as a great excuse to get to know her neighbors. She is crafty but does not have a lot of extra time. So she made holiday trail mix, placed it in decorative boxes, and wrote a note inviting her neighbors to her church's Christmas Eve worship celebration. She then sent out her husband to deliver the goods. And though none of her neighbors came to worship, every one of them now stops and talks to her and especially to her husband. That one act of love changed the atmosphere in her neighborhood. It was simple, and yet it made an impact on her and on others.

Christmas Miracle offerings are important, but they cannot replace the simple acts of love that Jesus calls us to do. Love more than writes a check; *love does.*

God, thank you for the opportunity to serve you and others through simple acts of love. Remind me on a daily basis how love, through the power of your Holy Spirit, can change the world. Amen.

Week 2

Down to Earth
Humility

6:

JANE

In your relationships with one another, have the same mindset as Christ Jesus: / Who, being in very nature God, / did not consider equality with God something to be used to his own advantage; / rather, he made himself nothing / by taking the very nature of a servant, / being made in human likeness. / And being found in appearance as a man, / he humbled himself / by becoming obedient to death—/ even death on a cross!

(Philippians 2:5-8)

In twenty-first-century America, Advent and Christmas are big business. In fact, our economy depends on consumers who buy, spend, and accumulate under the mantra, "'Tis the

Season." And I would be lying if I didn't admit that in the middle of all the lights, the music, and the mall, it's easy for me to be pulled into believing that the way to a better life is by getting more stuff.

Without fail, I'll see something while shopping and think to myself, *My daughter would love that* or *Dad has been talking about getting one of those—maybe I should buy it for him.* My need for more doesn't stop with shopping for others; at times I wonder what family and friends are going to buy for me. Not that I really want or need anything, but when someone thinks of me, even with the simplest of gifts, I feel loved. But some gifts evoke more than a feeling—some gifts change your perspective and remind you what emptying yourself really looks like.

Last Christmas season, I was handed a card by Jane. Jane catches me in the hallway each weekend, gives me a squeeze on the neck, and tells me an old, tired joke. She can get away with it, because she's seventy-nine years old. Jane is full of life and love, but she has limited resources—physically and financially. She has been widowed for years and needs friends to drive her back and forth to church. Luckily Jane befriended a neighbor who happened to attend Ginghamsburg.

Anyway, Jane handed me the card, and I opened it to discover two gifts: a newspaper clipping with an inspirational quote, and a check for ten dollars. It would have been disrespectful to tell Jane I could not accept the check, because in that moment I realized the sacrifice she had made to give one of her pastors a gift. She had very little, but out of that little she had given me a gift. It reminded me of Jesus' story about the widow's mite—the woman who understood that in giving herself and her life, she had the power to change the world.

I'm not sure I've met a human being with more joy than Jane. She is a weekly reminder that we don't need money, resources, or stuff to be full of joy. Jane has Jesus, and she tells me that's all she needs.

As we continue our journey through Advent, are we emptying ourselves of all the stuff that keeps us from having the mind of Christ?

Jesus, invade our lives with the Janes of the world. Remind us that joy cannot be purchased. It's a free gift, as long as we empty our hearts of fruitless desire and give you space to fill them. In your name. Amen.

7.

DOWNWARD
MOBILITY

*Jesus said to them, "You will drink the cup I drink
and be baptized with the baptism I am baptized
with, but to sit at my right or left is not for me to
grant. These places belong to those for whom they
have been prepared."*

(Mark 10:39-40)

Smug—that's how I would describe myself in my fifth-
grade Sunday school class. I was the kid who always had the
right answer. Not only was I pretty good at school, but I was
really good at learning this Jesus stuff. So in Sunday school I

made sure to be the first to volunteer, and of course the first to win any Bible competition we played. I can imagine how resentful my classmates must have been: "She thinks she's so smart!"; "Why can't she let someone else answer?"

I'll bet the disciples felt the same way about James and John. Here in Mark, they had just asked Jesus if they could sit in glory at his right and left—and they didn't ask off to the side where no one else could hear, but right in front of the other disciples. Talk about a bold move! I'm sure the other disciples must have been resentful: "Who do those two they think they are? Why them? Why not me?"

Sometimes in our need to achieve, to be the best, or to win the game, we make others resentful. Certainly I believe I am called to give God my very best—but I don't think my fifth-grade hubris was an example of my best. In fact, sometimes my need to win overshadows God's call to love. And then hurtful resentment follows.

We live in a world where winning and achieving are constantly being trumpeted. Best Buy has even told us we can "win the holidays." So Christmas is now a competition? I suspect we human beings can make it into such, but here Jesus reminds us, along with James and John, that our call is to discipleship—to follow Jesus no matter what the cost. It's not a call to our own honor and glory.

Could it be that this lesson is what God has been trying to teach us all along? When God came to earth and moved into our neighborhood, God demonstrated a down-to-earth humility that, at a glance, might have seemed weak when compared with first-century standards of glory and honor. For me and perhaps for you, the story of James and John holds up a mirror reminding us what our call to follow Jesus is all about: downward mobility, where we become second to God and to others. It's certainly not an invitation for people to walk all over us, but rather for us as human beings to become our best down-to-earth selves.

Sometimes my adult self has to remind my fifth-grade self that I win when others have the right answers; I win when those around me learn more about Jesus and the Bible; I win when fellow followers are honored for their faithful dedication to Jesus. Following Jesus is not about what we receive in the end, but about receiving what was intended for us from the beginning: God's gift of down-to-earth humility.

Lord, when I want to win, help me to see the consequences of my need to achieve. Challenge my need to be right or to win the game. Help me to receive your grace and humility as gift. Amen.

8.

GOD'S GIFT
OF SUCCESS

He did what was right in the eyes of the LORD, just as his father Amaziah had done. He sought God during the days of Zechariah, who instructed him in the fear of God. As long as he sought the LORD, God gave him success.

(2 Chronicles 26:4-5)

When King Uzziah was young, he did what his father had taught him to do: place his trust in God. And it worked pretty well for Uzziah, as today's Scripture reveals: because he sought the Lord, God gifted him with success. But as Uzziah gained wealth and political influence, he began to trust in his own ability to lead God's people into their future.

Now, before we leap to judge King Uzziah, let's recognize that it's easier to trust God if we're in over our heads. When Uzziah inherited his father's throne, he was a sixteen-year-old who needed all the help he could get; but his intense dependence on God waned as other voices became influential in his life. Finally Scripture tells us that "after Uzziah became powerful, his pride led to his downfall. He was unfaithful to the LORD his God" (2 Chronicles 26:16). You and I may not have anything like Uzziah's power and fame, but it doesn't take us long to stop trusting in God and start trusting in our own abilities.

Recently I've been trying to figure out how to maximize my time both at home and in my career. Sound familiar? I have charts, strategies, calendars, plans, and many a Pinterest board to help me out. A few days ago I sat down with a spiritual director to gain insight into how I could fall more in love with Jesus while remaining sane in commitments to my husband, children, and the church. During the session I explained that I had observed my own workaholic tendencies and tried to balance them with my deep commitment to spiritual disciplines and my desire to spend faithful time with my family.

I was feeling pretty good about what I had done, so I sort of expected an "'atta girl" from the spiritual director. Instead she said, "So, you've prayed about it!"

"Oh yes," I told her.

Then she asked a question that cut me to the heart: "What did God tell you?"

Even though I certainly had prayed, I wasn't sure I'd ever taken the time to listen. And I realized that my plans, strategies, and observations were just that—*my* plans, strategies, and observations.

You and I may not have the responsibility of running a kingdom, but all of us are responsible for our own lives. This Advent, as we actively await the birth of God's love come down to earth, I wonder if we're depending on our own abilities or if, instead, we're opening our ears and hearts to the voice of God in our lives. Maybe our success doesn't depend on how well we work but on how well we listen.

Lord God, in our hubris we plan, strategize, and strive for success. Remind us to stop spending precious energy and time striving, and open our hearts and ears to listen. In Jesus' name. Amen.

9.

A GIRL NAMED HAPPINESS

The Spirit of the Sovereign LORD is on me,
  because the LORD has anointed me
    to proclaim good news to the poor.
He has sent me to bind up the brokenhearted,
  to proclaim freedom for the captives
    and release from darkness for the prisoners.
      (Isaiah 61:1)

She stood in her mud hut, wide-eyed, which had me wondering if she had ever met a white person before. I had traveled to Swaziland, mostly to understand the work of

World Vision, not to meet a little girl. But there we were, face to face, me and a girl named Happiness.

Our group had spent days studying how Christian organizations over the years have attempted to move from forms of charity to movements of sustainability. Although Christians have done a lot of good in the name of Jesus, we also had caused a lot of harm and dependence in our attempts to be charitable. As a result, this was not your typical mission trip—we were not there to work or to build a house, a school, or even a church; rather, we were there to invest our time in building relationships. We went on the trip to meet people and to share our lives with people, so they could share their vision with us.

I did not go on that trip expecting to meet Happiness, a sponsor child. I'm not sure I even anticipated sponsoring a child. But there I was, facing the girl who would capture my family's heart.

I chose for us to sponsor Happiness because at the time she was younger than my daughter and older than my son, so she seemed a good fit for our family. She was quiet and reserved but full of life and wonder. She wanted to show me what she was learning in school. Honestly, I was surprised by her beautiful handwriting, given the fact that my four-year-old could not begin to write his name. Happiness and I spent a few hours together, talking, playing, laughing, and writing.

I had thought I was going to Swaziland to help save a people, but by the end of my time with her, this little girl had helped save me. She showed me that God had been alive and working in Swaziland long before my plane had ever arrived and would continue to work long after my plane left. She was a picture of God's good news.

It took me a while to explain to my kids that just because we sponsored Happiness, it didn't mean she would come to live with us. Finally, though, they realized that they had a friend, a sister in Christ they could write to, pray for, and grow up with, even though she lived halfway around the world. Through her, my children are learning that good news to the poor doesn't just mean the physically and economically poor, but also those of us who find ourselves spiritually deprived. That's why, each day right before school, we hold hands and pray for Happiness.

Happiness taught me that the gospel comes in many forms. Sometimes Jesus fashions himself into the hands of a little girl, who is delighted to show you how beautifully and proficiently she can write her name. And sometimes, in the unlikeliest of ways, Jesus shows us that the good news of the gospel is not about what we do but about the relationships we build.

Lord Jesus, I am grateful to witness your good news in Happiness, who reminds me that the gospel is not just to be lived but lived together in worldwide community. Amen.

10.

A PICTURE OF HUMILITY

Humble yourselves before the Lord, and he will lift you up.

(James 4:10)

Four times a year I travel to Cincinnati, Ohio, to the Transfiguration Spirituality Center (TSC). The TSC not only houses individuals and groups on retreat, but also is home to an Episcopal religious order for women. Each time I go there on retreat, I eat meals with the sisters, and some of the meals are in silence. For an extrovert who loves meeting new people, I found this practice annoying at first. However,

I soon learned that something happens in the silence. Not only do I find myself listening more intently, but my eyes are opened to what is happening around me.

These sisters care for one another carefully and intentionally. The eldest in the group is the feeblest, and although she is able to get her own plate of food, multiple sisters help her be seated and tend to her needs. Watching her, I see the humility baked into her daily choices—a common wardrobe worn for years, no signs of makeup or nail polish, a habit that covers her whitening hair. When I see her, I think to myself, "Could I ever be so humble as to lose my identity to Jesus?"

I walk in wearing heels, makeup, sometimes even ripped jeans. Seeing the simple garb of the sisters, my inner rebel screams out, "No way!" After all, my outward appearance expresses my identity, and these sisters are distinguishable only by the sizes and shapes of their faces and bodies. It seems like a grave sacrifice, losing their uniqueness to gain a closer connection with God and one another.

The humility in those decisions nearly takes my breath away. I ask myself, *How? Why?* As I continue to watch the sisters, I realize that when I'm near them, I feel joy and the presence of the holy. I don't believe it's because they are inherently holy; rather, their humility gives the Holy Spirit space to shine in and through them.

I don't believe Jesus is asking me to give up my favorite pair of jeans or shoes, but I do believe he asks me to hand over my identity for a new identity, an identity in which I and anyone else willing to follow Jesus are shaped and formed into their best selves, their best Spirit-filled selves. Inherent in the handoff is humility. The sisters are an invitation to a simpler life. Each time I visit, their humility calls me and challenges me to wrestle with my assumptions about what it means to follow Jesus.

In today's Scripture, James reminds us that humility is a prerequisite for being "lifted up." Glory is never the goal, but if we are lifted without humility, then the only thing people see is us. Humility reveals a deeper truth and identity. Humility is an invitation to a new way of living. I do not believe I will ever be called to live in a convent with a group of sisters, but I know they help shape my vision of what humility looks like.

What pictures of humility do you see? How can you spend time with people who challenge your vision of humility? What keeps you from handing your identity over to Jesus?

Lord Jesus, you are our ultimate picture of humility. Our pride so often keeps us from deepening our relationship with you and others. Help us to release our identity to you, so that we can fully experience our truest God-centered sselves. In your blessed name. Amen.

Week 3

Down to Earth
Lifestyle

11.

GOD-SIZED DREAMS

When Joseph woke up, he did what the angel of the Lord had commanded him and took Mary home as his wife.

(Matthew 1:24)

Dazed, confused, perhaps even wondering what he ate the night before, Joseph had a dream that was anything but comforting. In the dream, Joseph was asked to be the father of a child who was not his own and to believe that the child was supernaturally conceived by the Holy Spirit.

For Joseph, a man of honor and respect, it was a lot to swallow. Certainly it didn't represent Joseph's plan for his life or his future. But, as we learn in today's Scripture, Joseph did as he was told. In that moment, he was doing more than saying yes to God; he was saying yes to a different future. He knew that for years to come, he would have to live in the down-to-earth realities of everyday life: the suspicion, the rejection, the shame.

We can learn a lot from Joseph, not only about dreams but also about trust. Sometimes I think we Jesus followers have believed that God-sized dreams are easy, comfortable, and instantly manifested in our lives. I can remember as a teenager feeling a call to pastoral ministry, particularly preaching, and then not understanding why in a matter of months I was not the next Billy Graham. I could not see that God's dream for Rev. Graham was not God's dream for me; it was my picture of my future! Now here I am, decades later, realizing just how foolish my assumptions were about God dreams.

I doubt that I'm alone. You too may have pictures of your future that don't line up with your current life situation. Know that God wants to give you a new dream, not only for you but for the world. Throughout the Old and New Testaments, God's dreams not only change and challenge the dreamer but also God's people. In other words, our dreams are not our own.

When we step into those dreams, we are choosing to live a life of obedient discipleship. Discipleship costs us something. Jesus reminds us, "Whoever wants to be my disciple must deny themselves and take up their cross daily and follow me. For whoever wants to save their life will lose it, but whoever loses their life for me will save it" (Luke 9:23-24). Stepping into God-sized dreams will cost us: comfort, ease, and our picture of our future.

Comfort, ease, and his picture of his future were what God, in the dream, asked Joseph to give up. It was no small ask, but because Joseph had the courage and faith to say yes, he was father to the Savior of the world. His faith, his fathering, his life were poured into Jesus—he discipled Jesus. Joseph's obedience changed everything.

I'm not Billy Graham, because God has a different and unique dream for me and for you. As you prepare for the birth of Jesus, when God comes down to earth, what picture of your future is God asking you to give up and what God-dream is coming to life inside you? What obstacles, bumps, and barriers do you anticipate along the way: family expectations, unspoken rules, uncomfortable pictures for your future?

Like Joseph, we may awaken a little dazed and confused, but with the power of the Holy Spirit on our side we can live into a God-sized future.

God, pour out your Holy Spirit into our minds and hearts so that we can dream God-sized dreams whether asleep or awake. In Jesus' name. Amen.

12.

UNCLAIMED GIFTS

"Truly I tell you, if you have faith as small as a mustard seed, you can say to this mountain, 'Move from here to there,' and it will move. Nothing will be impossible for you."

(Matthew 17:20)

In Chapter 3 of *Down to Earth*, Mike Slaughter tells the story of how he failed to redeem a gift card I had given him. Don't feel bad, Mike. You're not alone, as this story will show.

I not only give gift cards; I receive them—a lot. In fact, though my mother struggles to give them to me, it's my preferred gift. But a few months ago I was in an airport, standing in line at Starbucks, when I looked in my purse and saw them—two unredeemed Starbucks cards. Truth be told, I didn't know how long they had been in my wallet. Perhaps they had been gifts from the previous Christmas. Since I drink a lot of coffee, I assumed there couldn't be more than a few dollars on each of the cards; they might even be all used up. I was wrong, really wrong. I had fifty dollars of unredeemed Starbucks cards in my wallet! That's a whole lot of coffee! It wasn't even my first visit to Starbucks on that trip. Frustrated, I was determined to use every single penny on those cards before I paid any more cash at Starbucks.

As Mike points out in his chapter, "We have too often failed to redeem what has already been paid for with a price!" But this time Mike isn't talking about gift cards. He's talking about the gift of faith.

In today's Scripture, Jesus reminds the people listening that if they have faith the size of a mustard seed, they can tell a mountain to move and it will move. Faith is a powerful force—not necessarily because people have power, but because when we act in faith, we give the Holy Spirit room to move. When the Spirit moves, people and lives are changed.

It's easy for us to claim we have faith, but, like the fifty dollars' worth of unredeemed Starbucks cards, most of the time it stays in our pockets and does not see the light of day. Mike says it this way: "It is just too easy to hold to a form of faith and yet at the same time to deny faith's power." He reminds us that every miracle has two components: divine intervention + human responsibility. In other words, it's not just on God; it's also on you and me.

But here's the good news: there is something about this time of the year that makes people more spiritually sensitive. Even nonreligious or nominally religious folk sing Christmas carols and buy gifts for their friends and families. The way that I see it, it's an opportunity for followers of Jesus to exercise their faith—to cash in their cards and visibly see the movement of God.

Where in your life could you use a little faith? What do you see in your neighborhood or community that could use faith in action? What miracle are you partnering with God to create?

Miraculous God, may I never hold on to a form of faith and deny its power. You have paid the price; let me put my faith and trust in you. In Jesus' name. Amen.

13.

EMPTY HOUSE,
FULL HEART

*Then he said, 'This is what I'll do. I will tear down
my barns and build bigger ones, and there I will
store my surplus grain. And I'll say to myself, "You
have plenty of grain laid up for many years. Take
life easy; eat, drink and be merry."'*

(Luke 12:18-19)

My Uncle Mick threw the best Christmas parties. Every
year he held a Christmas open house. Preparations for
the open house began in November. There were forty-six
Christmas trees to decorate and thousands of lights that

covered his house. Mick loved Christmas, and he enjoyed the awe and wonder of each person as they walked through his Christmas wonderland of a home. Mick loved Christmas so much, he kept a decorated Christmas tree in his bedroom so that he could wake up to Christmas every morning! And although my uncle's passion for Christmas was admirable, it became, for me, a picture of how our lives and possessions are temporary.

In today's Scripture, Jesus tells the story of a successful man who decided to build bigger barns to keep up with his bumper crop. The man had looked to the future and decided to invest in his own wealth. Sounds reasonable, except that all his work and investment soon showed itself to be glaringly temporary, because the very next day the man died. My uncle, that fun-loving and generous man, died and died young. And what had taken him all those years to collect—lights, trees, and all—was sold in one day at auction. I still can remember that day, each hour seeing customer after happy customer carrying away my uncle's favorite things: bubble lights, plastic reindeer, boxes upon boxes of Santas. When the day was over, nothing was left and the house was empty. The picture was sad and unsettling.

At the time, I collected Anchor Hocking's Ruby Red glassware, a hobby my uncle had introduced me to when I was sixteen. I stopped collecting the day after the auction. The picture was too real—we brought nothing into the world and will take nothing with us when we leave. That empty house changed the way I live and how I invest my time and resources.

Advent is a season for us to remember and reevaluate what matters most in our lives—the stuff or the people? Do we spend our holiday season worrying about presents for people we may not even like, purchasing stuff they may not need, all because we think it's what we're supposed to do? Or do we follow God's way, a new way to live?

I will always be grateful for the contagious way that Uncle Mick celebrated Christmas: his laugh, his singing, his parties. He loved Christmas, but he also loved people. I'm grateful that in his death he taught me a lesson: stuff without relationship is just stuff.

As Mick himself might have said, "Fill your life with people, and when you die your house may be empty but your heart will be full." I am looking to die with a full heart.

God, we are grateful for the people who have been in our lives who have lived and died well. May they remind us that we are merely the temporary stewards of all of our stuff, and that our lives' worth comes from our relationship with you and with others. In Jesus' name. Amen.

14.

JESUS WAS A REFUGEE

When they had gone, an angel of the Lord appeared to Joseph in a dream. "Get up," he said, "take the child and his mother and escape to Egypt. Stay there until I tell you, for Herod is going to search for the child to kill him."

(Matthew 2:13)

At Ginghamsburg Church we expect thousands of our friends, neighbors, and even strangers to come celebrate Christmas Eve with us. Since many of those folk do not know who we are or anything about our church, one might expect that we don't talk about anything controversial at those services.

But this is Ginghamsburg, and this year God gave Pastor Mike Slaughter a vision for mobilizing churches across the country to give aid to the plight of refugees worldwide. It turns out that nearly 1 in every 122 human beings on the face of the planet is a displaced person, whether because of natural disaster, the threat of violence, or a shortage of resources.

Many people don't know it, but Jesus himself was a refugee. He and his family spent two years fleeing the violence of King Herod, a man who mandated that every boy in the region under the age of two be executed. We call this genocide, and no matter where we fall on the political spectrum, it's a tragedy that has lasted from Jesus' time to ours.

So on Christmas Eve, I watched whole sections of our worship celebration be dedicated to reminding people that Jesus was a refugee, and refugees around the world need our help. Participating in worship, I found that I was uncomfortable and at times irritated that we would highlight such a controversial subject when people just wanted to sing "Silent Night" and go home. But I also was grateful to be part of a team that had the courage to share the story and stand up for refugees. As I learned later, many people worshiping that night found the experience powerful and moving, but some just wanted to have a Christmas Eve "without dead babies."

When you think about it, that's probably what God wants too: a Christmas Eve without the threat of daily violence, a Christmas Eve without the bodies of toddlers washing up on shore, a Christmas Eve when children are not forced to ride on bus tops to escape drug cartels, a Christmas Eve with no cancer, a Christmas Eve when the people we love don't die, a Christmas Eve when all the followers of Jesus truly find peace on earth as it is in heaven. God's heart breaks for all the people suffering throughout the world—those sitting in seats in our worship celebration and those thousands of miles away in camps for displaced persons.

Brothers and sisters, following Jesus is uncomfortable, inconvenient, and at times irritating, but Jesus never said it would be easy. What makes your heart break? Where do you see God's heart breaking? Where is God calling you to become uncomfortable, irritated, and inconvenienced?

Jesus, you were a refugee, and you experienced the threat of violence. Break our hearts for the displaced persons throughout the world. Help us to be irritated, inconvenienced, and uncomfortable this Advent and Christmas season. In your blessed name. Amen.

15.

A LIFESTYLE OF SERVICE

When he had finished washing their feet, he put on his clothes and returned to his place. "Do you understand what I have done for you?" he asked them. "You call me 'Teacher' and 'Lord,' and rightly so, for that is what I am. Now that I, your Lord and Teacher, have washed your feet, you also should wash one another's feet."

(John 13:12-14)

I'm not afraid of washing feet. In fact, with two boys at home I've scrubbed my share of dirty toes. But footwashing may not have the same cultural relevance as it did in Jesus' day.

For Jesus, when he gathered with his disciples at the Last Supper, he first washed their feet. It seemed shocking and made the disciples uncomfortable, which may have been why Jesus did it. By washing their feet, he was calling them to do the same for each other. But of course his actions weren't about feet or even footwashing. They were visual reminders that as his followers, we are to be servants first, even if (or especially if) we are leaders in the church. So, what does footwashing look like in the twenty-first century? Maybe it's like More Than Carpenters.

I ran across a friend of mine one evening at a Kingdom Investors Meeting, a gathering time for church leaders who invest their time and resources into the movement we call Ginghamsburg Church. That night I learned that my friend was part of a group called More Than Carpenters, a ministry started by people who wanted to use carpentry, plumbing, welding, and other gifts to serve people inside the church and throughout the community. The ministry had taken a while to get off the ground. Even though the members had possessed the resources of skill and time (many were retired), their ministry was just not taking shape.

But then something happened. The ministry leader, Doug Powell, read a book called *When Helping Hurts*, by Steve Corbett and Brian Fikkert, and realized that if their ministry was to help the community, it could not be merely a handout, but a hand up. With this in mind, Doug and his group established some criteria—each person they helped had to contribute to the project. Sometimes the contribution was financial; other times, the person bought materials for someone else—a new wheelchair ramp for an elderly woman, a new drain for someone's sink.

It also meant an invitation to participate in the work. Instead of simply doing work for others, the men and women in More Than Carpenters committed themselves to teaching individuals and families the basics of plumbing, heating, carpentry, and anything else that would contribute a long-term solution to a short-term problem.

Finally, the group came to believe that Jesus was calling them to share God's good news—through praying with others, getting to know someone's story, and, if the opportunity arose, unapologetically inviting these persons into a saving relationship with Jesus Christ. The new framework changed everything. Before, they were struggling to get their ministry off the ground; now more than fifty people are serving the community through their More Than Carpenters ministry. These men and women are using the gifts of their hands, bringing resources to people who are in need of their gifts and, in turn, teaching the community about our interdependence with one another.

They have learned learned that service is more than a one-time act. It is more than projects. Service is a way of life.

Jesus used a bowl of water and a towel to serve his disciples. What gifts can you use this Advent season to serve the people around you?

Servant God, continue to remind us of your simple acts of love and service. Throughout Advent, help us to carve time out of our schedules to serve the people in our homes, churches, and communities. In Jesus' name. Amen.

Week 4

Down to Earth
Obedience

16.

DRIVING WITHOUT
A BUMPER

*Therefore, my dear friends, as you have always
obeyed—not only in my presence, but now much
more in my absence—continue to work out your
salvation with fear and trembling, for it is God
who works in you to will and to act in order to
fulfill his good purpose.*

(Philippians 2:12-13)

One icy, snowy Saturday afternoon, I was hanging out at
home with my best friend, Sarah. We had just watched *The
Breakfast Club* and were determined to return the movie on
time. (This was before the days of Redbox and Netflix.) My
mom wasn't home, so I called to tell her we'd be venturing out

into the winter weather. She told me in no uncertain terms to stay off the icy roads.

Now, I was a young driver but not a new driver, and I deemed myself perfectly capable of navigating the icy roadways in order to avoid paying the late fee. I figured that if I was careful, we could return the movie and my mother would never be the wiser.

So, Sarah and I piled into my dirty turquoise 1996 Dodge Shadow. Oh, did I mention that we lived in the Hocking Hills, a neighborhood with an elevation change of nearly one thousand feet between my house and the rental store?

As we drove through the falling snow, we slowed down to twenty-five miles an hour, just to be sure we'd make it to the rental store safely. One mile into the journey, the car began to slide off into a ditch. In what seemed like a slow motion movie—not *The Breakfast Club*—the car turned 180 degrees, slipped off the road, and landed with the back bumper in a snow bank. Sarah and I jumped from the car, ran around to see if there was any damage, and decided everything looked good.

Yes, I thought to myself, *there's still a chance I will not get caught.*

With no cell phone and no house in sight, we prayed that someone would come to our rescue and that it would not be anyone who knew my parents. In minutes, a neighbor stopped by and offered to drag us out of the ditch. He got a rope from his pickup truck, tied it to our front axle, and pulled us out. The car came out of the snow, but the bumper did not. In a matter of minutes it had frozen to the icy bank, and now we were forced to dig it out.

With the help of my neighbor we made it back home, put the car in the driveway, and confronted the fact that we would have to pay the late fee. Worst yet, I would be caught. Evidence of my disobedience lay crumpled next to the garage door. When my mom arrived home, I received my punishment: I had to drive that Dodge Shadow without a bumper until I could afford to pay five hundred dollars for a new one. It was a steep price tag for a young adult who had a limited income.

My parents wanted me to understand that obedience is not about avoiding punishment; rather, it's about saying *yes* to the right action. They forced me to experience the consequences of my poor choice.

Today I'm an adult, but often I wonder if I really learned that lesson. Sometimes I still think of obedience as avoiding punishment, rather than saying *yes* to the right action. As a result, I've carried home a lot of "bumpers."

Perhaps you've had similar experiences in your life. Maybe you're carrying around a few bumpers yourself. God wants to work in your life and mine so God's purpose can be filled in and through us.

So, when facing the icy roads of life, remember how ugly a car looks without a bumper.

Lord God, obedience is not the avoidance of punishment, but an opportunity for you to fulfill your good purpose in us and through us. Help me say yes to obedience. In Jesus' name. Amen.

17.

YOUR BIG YES

"I am the Lord's servant," Mary answered. "May your word to me be fulfilled." Then the angel left her.

(Luke 1:38)

All of us face tough decisions. Many of the folks who come to me for pastoral support are asking the fundamental question, "How do I make the right decision?" And not just the "right" decision, but one that's in alignment with God's wishes for their lives and for the world.

When I talk to people about these things, sometimes I wish the Bible had a "magic eight ball" power, where we could shake open its pages and all the answers to life's tough questions would fall out.

"Should I apply for a new job?" we ask.

"Outcome looks favorable," says Jesus.

But faith does not work that way. So, when facing a tough choice, how do we decide?

We can go to the Bible, but the answer isn't always clear. Even with Mary's story in today's Scripture, the Bible only gives a highlight reel. We don't get every detail of what happened or even of Mary's inner dialogue. Sometimes when we read through stories like this one, we get the false impression that faith-filled decisions can or should be made in a flash. I don't believe that's the case. Our biggest "yeses" deserve our best time. If that's true, then how do we find the time to make a good decision, to say a big yes?

For me, life's toughest choices typically aren't between the bad and good, but between the good and good. And so I have employed a little guide over the years when facing those choices. The guide is a series of questions.

Have I prayed?

I'm a follower of Jesus and a pastor, so prayer is assumed, right? Not always. Sometimes worry and anxiety crowd out my prayer life, and I make a decision just to quiet the noise in my head—out of fear or frustration rather than faith. Praying gives me time and perspective, two things I need to make a solid choice.

Have I listened?

Just because I pray doesn't mean I listen to what God is saying. Listening is difficult for me, and so I genuinely have to ask out loud, "Am I really listening?"

Have I talked to Jon?

Jon is my husband, so for me this question is about consulting the person whose life is most deeply affected by my decision. For you it might be a significant other, family member, or friend. I find that people I love and trust can help me see challenges or pitfalls that I would not otherwise see.

Have I taken the leap?

At the end of the day, making decisions means taking a leap. And with the leap, we must own the decision. Truly owning it is why decision-making is so difficult in the first place. God has given us an incredible power to choose.

The next time you are face-to-face with a tough choice—between good and bad or maybe between good and good—try using this little guide. It doesn't always work, but it will give you a better chance of being in sync with God and with your loved ones.

God, pour out your Spirit over us. Open our hearts to feel, our ears to listen, and our hands to serve you. Help us to pause and listen to you when faced with life's biggest decisions. In Jesus' name. Amen.

18.

A STORY WORTH TELLING

*The LORD said, "I have indeed seen the misery of
my people in Egypt. I have heard them crying out
because of their slave drivers, and I am concerned
about their suffering. So I have come down to rescue
them from the hand of the Egyptians and to bring
them up out of that land into a good and spacious
land, a land flowing with milk and honey."*

(Exodus 3:7-8a)

Sometimes my children whine about our Christmas
practices. They remind me, even though Christmas is not our
birthday, that Conner on the bus received nineteen presents

this year, or that Sarah had so many gifts she couldn't count them all. In these moments, one part of me wants to give Conner and Sarah's parents a piece of my mind, but I restrain myself, realizing that some of the stories may have been exaggerated and that those other families may not share the same story as our family.

In fact it's the story that matters. Each Christmas morning as the Billups children climb out of bed, they are as excited as any child to experience the awe and wonder of Christmas. But instead of receiving mounds of presents each Christmas, our children receive one and only one. (It's only in our later years that my husband, Jon, and I have realized the economic genius of this practice—it certainly serves our budget well.) In our family, Christmas isn't about gift giving; it's about storytelling.

Instead of opening gifts the first thing on Christmas morning, our family shares the Christmas story. We have years of children's books that tell the story in unique ways, and sometimes we use Nativity sets so our kids can participate in the story. After telling the story we pray, giving God thanks for the gift of Jesus, God's Son come down to earth through God's grace and love.

Now, I would be lying if I didn't admit that my kids are bursting with anticipation, because just like any children they can't wait to see what has arrived under the Christmas tree. But even in those moments, we make sure the children open their presents one by one, taking their time and enjoying the gifts they receive. Finally the morning ends with a breakfast feast, prepped the night before and baked while we tell the story. When we sit down to eat, we share our Christmas memories—what Christmas was like when we were children and the impact our families had on us during the Christmas season.

Mary, too, had a story, of a God who delivered her people from captivity in Egypt to freedom in the Promised Land. Mary had a deliverer God who heard the cries of the people. I want to help our children realize that, like Mary, we have a story that shapes the way we understand the world. Our story and our collective memory shape us, changing the way we celebrate Christmas.

As a Jesus follower, I realize that as I raise my children I am making disciples. As their parents, my husband and I are the first to tell them the story that has shaped our lives and will continue to shape theirs.

As your people, God, we have a story that is worth sharing. Grant us the opportunity to share your story with the generations that surround us. In Jesus' name. Amen.

19.

CAN YOU SEE
THE LIGHT?

The true light that gives light to everyone was coming into the world.

(John 1:9)

Sometimes Christmas Eve seems to be filled with anything but light. Some of us have parties to attend, others have family obligations, still others need to stay up half the night assembling Christmas toys. And let's not forget making sure the milk and cookies are prepped and we've put out the reindeer food!

Even for us church professionals, the night before Christmas can seem like a marathon, often with multiple services and celebrations. At times it becomes an evening to endure rather than a celebration to enjoy.

And yet, there's something holy about celebrating Christmas Eve at church. Perhaps it's the warmth of families gathering, or how loud congregation sings, or the faces you don't see at other times during the year. Whatever it is, each Christmas Eve celebration is alive with anticipation.

Sometimes we preacher types think it matters what clever thing we can say about the birth of Jesus. Most of the time I remind our team, and myself, "Let's make sure we simply tell the story."

But no matter how moving the message or powerful the music, here are the real essentials of Christmas Eve: we'd better sing "Silent Night," and we'd better light some candles.

What's up with the candles? Is there a secret pyromaniac dwelling inside each of us? I believe the real passion for lighting candles on Christmas Eve comes in the proclamation that is today's Scripture: "The true light that gives light to everyone was coming into the world." Standing in the darkened sanctuary, we realize the impact of one light, then two, three, four, and so many more. Suddenly, seeing the place light up, the spreading of the gospel, God's good news, makes perfect sense. This story, our story, is contagious! The light is shared, along with the warmth within us. We are part of God's evolving story.

Christmas is a story of hope. When we gather for Christmas celebrations, that hope is clearly proclaimed when each man, woman, and child lights a small wand of wax. Of course, it's not the church tradition that is holy, but the way the candles make Christ's message clear, simple, and tangible for even the youngest person in the room. Lighting the candles answers God's question, "Can you see my light?"

Not every person celebrates the night before Christmas in a church, but I believe all of us have the opportunity to see the light. This Advent season, as you prepare to celebrate Christmas Eve at home or at church, take the time to read the story, light a candle (or several), and proclaim the promise: God's light has come down to earth, where it shines in us and through us.

Light of the World, come, pour out your light and love over us. May we share your light with all we encounter until the whole world has been touched by your love. Lord Jesus, thank you for simple traditions that make tangible the hope you bring in our lives. In your name. Amen.

20.

CHRISTMAS
ALL YEAR LONG

*Do everything readily and cheerfully—no bicker-
ing, no second-guessing allowed! Go out into the
world uncorrupted, a breath of fresh air in this
squalid and polluted society. Provide people with a
glimpse of good living and of the living God.*
                    (Philippians 2:14-15 The Message*)*

Sometimes I'm a little cynical when it comes to the insti-
tution we call the church. Maybe it's my inner Scrooge, but
too often I've met folk in the church who have let bitterness,
arguments, and tension pervade their lives. And though the
children's song says, "If you're happy and you know it, your

face will surely show it," the faces of the faithful do not always express happiness, let alone joy. At times like that, when I feel I can't take any more cynicism, I go looking for genuine expressions of joy—the spirit of Christmas.

One Friday afternoon, the Scrooge within started to take over, and so I decided to go on an adventure. "God," I prayed, "lead me to someone who loves Jesus and wants to talk about it." For about a half hour I drove around the booming metropolis of Tipp City, Ohio, population 11,000. I made a few stops at churches and had brief conversations, but I didn't get the opportunity to take the conversations further.

Finally I gave up on the adventure and decided to shop for a coffee mug at the Hotel Gallery in downtown Tipp City. There I ran into one of the owners, whose name was Steve. I introduced myself, told him what I was looking for, and he helped me find it. But he didn't stop there. He asked me where I lived and what brought me downtown. As we talked, I discovered Steve's passion for what he called "Jesus and the marketplace." Steve shared with me his vision for uniting what we do behind the four walls of church with what people do every day of their lives, creating a space in which "faith collides with the places where people work and play."

Before I realized it, we were walking all over downtown Tipp City. Steve described the history of our town, as well as what he believed God wanted to do in and through partnerships with churches, businesses, and people. I was inspired, I was energized, and I realized I had found what I was looking for—a breath of fresh air, a contagious faith, a person full of the Christmas spirit. And it wasn't even Christmas!

I walked out of the Hotel Gallery that day on a mission: How can the church be a breath of fresh air to the world—creative, inspiring, innovative, and contagious? How can we share the spirit of Christmas all year long?

That chance encounter with Steve led to a partnership with the hotel and other churches in Tipp City. It was a reminder of the Spirit's power to bring new life not only to those far from faith, but also those like me who sometimes find our faith becoming a little crusty.

Come, fresh wind. Come, Holy Spirit. Breathe life into our lives so that we can feel joy in the presence of the people around us. Amen.